JUST DANCE

Spotlight on
Ballroom

Hannah Gramson

Lerner Publications ◆ Minneapolis

For Abby and Lucy

Lerner Publications Company
An imprint of Lerner Publishing Group, Inc.
241 First Avenue North
Minneapolis, MN 55401 USA

For reading levels and more information, look up this title at www.lernerbooks.com.

Main body text set in Mikado.
Typeface provided by HVD.

Editor: Annie Zheng **Designer:** Mary Ross
Lerner team: Martha Kranes

Library of Congress Cataloging-in-Publication Data

Names: Gramson, Hannah, author.
Title: Spotlight on ballroom / Hannah Gramson.
Description: Minneapolis, MN : Lerner Publications Company, [2024] | Series: Lerner sports rookie. Just dance | Includes bibliographical references and index. | Audience: Ages 5–8 years | Audience: Grades K–1 | Summary: "Ballroom dancers spin, twirl, and kick out their legs. Readers will enjoy learning all about the world of ballroom dance, including what to wear, how to compete, and how to get started"– Provided by publisher.
Identifiers: LCCN 2023038390 (print) | LCCN 2023038391 (ebook) | ISBN 9798765625651 (lib. bdg.) | ISBN 9798765628836 (pbk.) | ISBN 9798765634004 (epub)
Subjects: LCSH: Ballroom dancing–Juvenile literature. | Ballroom dancers–Juvenile literature. | Dance–Competitions–Juvenile literature.
Classification: LCC GV1751 .G75 2024 (print) | LCC GV1751 (ebook) | DDC 793.3/3–dc23/eng/20231018

LC record available at https://lccn.loc.gov/2023038390
LC ebook record available at https://lccn.loc.gov/2023038391

Manufactured in the United States of America
1-1010138-51899-12/21/2023

Table of Contents

Chapter 1
Welcome to Ballroom Dance

A couple glides across the dance floor. They turn, dip, and kick. This is ballroom dance.

Ballroom dance is a popular dance style. You can watch competitions on TV. There are four major ballroom dance styles. These are smooth, rhythm, standard, and Latin.

★ **Fun Fact** ★

The cha-cha is a Latin dance. It started in Cuba.

Chapter 2
Getting Started

Ballroom dancers wear many types of shoes. Some dancers wear dress shoes. Some wear heels.

Ballroom dancers perform in a large room. Ballroom events often take place in a dance hall.

You will need a partner. Ballroom dances are done by two people.

★ **Fun Fact** ★

The longest tango ever danced lasted almost two days!

Chapter 3
Leading and Following

Partners are divided into leaders and followers. Leaders decide the speed and what steps to do. Followers follow their speed and steps.

You can choose to be a leader or a follower. But remember to respect your partner. Good partners listen to each other.

★ Up Close! ★

How Leaders Do a Hesitation

- Hold your partner's hands.
- Step forward with your right foot.
- Bring your left foot forward.
- Go up on your toes.
- Come back down.

Chapter 4
Put on a Show!

Ballroom dancers can practice for fun or for competition. In a competition, dancers perform in front of judges.

Dancers are scored based on their skill. They're also judged on how well they work together.

★ **Tip** ★
Good posture is important.

21

All ballroom dances are fun!
Find a partner and get started.

Glossary

competition: an event or contest where people compete

posture: how a person positions their body

tango: a type of international standard ballroom dance

Learn More

Becker, Trudy. *Swing Dance*. Mendota Heights, MN: Little Blue Readers, 2023.

Hammond, Mel. *Spotlight on Ballet*. Minneapolis: Lerner Publications, 2025.

Robbins, Dean. *¡Mambo mucho mambo! The Dance That Crossed Color Lines*. Somerville, MA: Candlewick, 2021.

Index

Photo Acknowledgments

Image credits: tarczas/Shutterstock, p. 5; AP Photo/Hendrik Schmidt, p. 7; sportpoint/Getty Images, p. 9; AP Photo/TopPhoto, p. 11; Anton Gvozdikov/Shutterstock, p. 13; JackF/Getty Images, p. 15; Tutti Frutti/Shutterstock, p. 17; avevizavi_com/Shutterstock, p. 19; Alex Bogatyrev/Shutterstock, p. 21; fizkes/Getty Images, p. 23.
Design elements: Kilroy79/Getty Images; Iuliia Mashinets/Getty Images.
Cover: AP Photo/Eugene Hoshiko.